LANGUAGE OF BIRDS

ANON EDITION

2020
Flagstaff New York

LANGUAGE OF BIRDS

Texts
Allan Graubard

Images
Rik Lina

Content design Thom Burns
On the cover *Bird Castle:* oil painting by Rik Lina
ISBN: 978-0-9761436-7-3

CONTENTS

Mr. Lina's works in this volume are done in a variety of media including ink, pastel, acrylic resin, pigment, oil paint and a leaf.

Language of Birds

Argument

The phrase, "language of birds" has a peculiar history marked by different authors from various traditions. But whether an author hailed from old Scandinavia, ancient India, classical Greece, medieval Persia and Africa, renaissance Europe, or modern America, the phrase carries a longing common to our species: that language is generative of thought, emotion, and culture and what we lack in the way we live language can revive and restore. Whether this occurs materially or immaterially does not matter; the effect is all. From apparent realities come hidden resources inclusive of other species. So we listen, seeking our place from the sounds we hear and those we sense in the great, lyrically cacophonous, ever sensuous chorus of birds.

What natural succor by sound, ever present and affective, has graced our lives more than bird song? What ties us so inextricably to the larger composites in which we live—rushing wind, falling rain, crashing thunder—than this same singing; surging and receding, evaporating and returning as if torqued by its own transient moon? What can't we gain from what we have so near and take so much for granted, allies, hunters, and prey?

Counter Argument

The "language of birds" is a ruse to capture the unwary when touring the outer precincts of symbolism. Part literary metaphor or hermetic proposition, birdsong, however lovely it is, does little to satisfy the grandiose terms applied to it: key to Adamic language, the secret principle of high poetics, a source from which language evolves from homonymic rapture. As Nicosa of Palermo put it—this 16th century critic of neo-Platonism who espoused the same principles though he never could admit it: "birds sing because they must, not because they seek what we imagine they do."

The evocation of a Nightingale as a vehicle for hermetic knowledge is an invention, as purposeless as it is pale when contrasted to the vibrant mimicry of this exceptional creature.

"Beware of the shadows that flicker across Plato's cave," Nicosa warns. The realities they suggest in the natural order of things and beings have little relation to what our senses reveal by day.

The Symbol

An older Persian sailor I met once years ago when I was much younger told me this tale. It made an impression on me then. Perhaps because of the way he told it, sitting on an empty packing crate smoking his pipe on the far end of a dock that curved into the bay. As I remember it, there wasn't anyone else about that morning. He asked me the time as I passed him. I wasn't wearing a watch and couldn't go any farther. So we started to chat. Then for some reason—I can't say why, he began:

"Funny, not knowing who you are. Have I ever...? A name... first and last; like you... Parents... sure... A sister who died early... Don't recall much about her... Her smell mostly... Clean and salty, like it is here... School friends... Although I wasn't much of a student... Women, a few women... before I met my wife... We were happy enough... I worked the river barge and was never gone for more than a week... Children? Either she was barren or I was sterile... We never found out. No point. And after a while, it didn't matter. We had each other and our tight little circle...

"She fell ill... Fever took hold, dug into her and didn't let go... The doctors... They did what they could... I was up river working the barge when the call came... She was most everything I wanted... So after the funeral, scattering her ashes, all of them, I couldn't bear the thought of keeping her with me, I quit the routine.

"Learned radio and Morse and got my papers... Sold the furniture and whatever else I could... Signed up for the merchant marine... That was a decent job... Took care of the ship's communications and all that business and, now and then, sat at the captain's table with the other officers... I'd work my shift, check in with my mates, walk the deck and hit the hay... I missed my wife... Guess I learned to live with it, as I could...

"Perhaps I was bored or fed up. Perhaps I was driven to it. Perhaps she was there in the back of my mind urging me to do something different, 'something silly,' as she called it... But when we docked in Sitter, I'd had it... I walked down that plank with a small suitcase and didn't return. The ship departed, my name on report... Could I work again? I didn't know and didn't care. I had some savings, enough to go pretty far in this country, and wasn't all that concerned about where I would live either...

"I traveled inland by train and horse, exploring here and there, no plan, just where I wanted to go, and stopped finally in a small village halfway up a lush low mountain with the jungle spread out below. I suppose I was tired of moving around. Once the place had tourists, not many, enough to keep a hotel in business but that was years before. Still, it was there, with its few simple rooms. Oh, it was comfortable enough for a guy like me; getting on in years. Was it a month I stayed; a bit more? Something like that. I'd look about that room with its bed, desk, chair, and an old weathered armoire and wonder what my life might have been if she hadn't died.

"Every morning just before dawn a Nightingale went at it. The other birds were asleep, sunk into their feathers, resting just enough so they could flit about during the day, eating and feeding their young, protecting their turf when they had to. Doing what birds do to stay alive.

"Was this Nightingale any different? I only know he sang his little heart out. Not that he had a particular song. He didn't. I knew he was a Nightingale because he sang so many different songs. Somehow, he stored up the songs he heard from other birds. And when he didn't have to compete with them, when it was real quiet, still dark, he began.

"I'd listen to him in a half sleep there on that bed, perfectly content, charmed; as if my wife were alive in those songs; as if all the little chance events that brought me here fell into place; this place where I was; where I should be.

"I knew the Nightingale didn't sing for me but it sure felt that way. A kind of composite bird, made up of all the songs he took from other birds, and which he sang as night began to lift, the horizon going pale and then fog... that just-before-dawn wispy fog, which stuck around until the sun burned it off.

"His songs fell into me, filling me up, transporting me out of that poor hotel halfway up the side of that low lush valley with its family farms and goats and cattle and quiet local markets... a rural makeshift school... a community center always in repair...

"However trivial it sounds, I loved it. And everything about the place...

"Then that was that. I'd used up my funds. So I trekked back to the port city. The same place I jumped ship in. Found another job easy enough; radioman on a ship from a different company. They didn't seem to care that I appeared just like that with my papers. They needed to fill a position. Hired me on the spot. If you were competent and certified, that was enough then.

"Just like that Nightingale, when all the other birds were silent..."

Glissando

The song arcs into the high registers, tremulously narrowing in pitch as if, with Icarus wings, it seeks its fate in expiration and silence. It hovers, shifting slightly, and through it—faint, low—a bass echo thrums in distant ghostly counter-pitch. The self-made duet conspires, respires, softly unrolls, recalibrates, sharpens, stutters; minute feathery seismograph that satiates and transpires, ever then, always now, in the radiant heart of hearing.

Glissando by Nightingale is its name, this bird who rests as the other birds wake...

Bird Land

He was living in an empty place full of birds. Somehow, he had walked here, walking and walking, stopping when tired, sleeping when he could walk no more. He had come from another place but the memory of that place, the feeling of that place in his memory, had left him. He did not regret the journey. He did not remember how long the journey had taken. He only knew that when he began it, he couldn't do otherwise. He had to leave, to walk, and then, after a long, exhausting period of walking, arrive.

This was his place now, which he shared with birds; one man in a new place full of birdsong, of quick feathery flashes, of playful and deadly aggression, of nesting and hunting, of flocking at dawn and dusk, those great aerial masses of swirling, swooping, ascending bodies formed by a shared sensibility of flight.

He closed his eyes and opened them. He was still in this place of birds that spread to each horizon, and which, other than trees and bushes, fields and slow rolling hills speckled with streams, rivulets and ponds, was empty.

Then he was hungry and thirsty. He hadn't eaten or drunk in a long while, ever since he began walking. And while water was available, perhaps there was fruit, berries or mushrooms. Perhaps he would find a dead bird, start a fire with twigs then build it up with branches, and cook the bird over it; singeing and stripping off the feathers, until he could eat it - flesh, bones, and organs.

He would find what he needed and keep himself alive as long as he stayed here, as long as it was necessary for him to stay, having come from a place he didn't recall, a past he didn't feel, a life he had lost to this empty place full of birds.

A long time passed. He didn't know how long. He had explored this place whose extent never diminished, whose borders were ever distant, which seemed to expand as he traversed it, and found enough food and water to sustain him. Sometimes he was happy, other times sad. Sometimes he was lonely, other times he listened to the birds and watched them, bored or fascinated by their antics, their daring and struggles and conflicts and losses and triumphs. And now and then he would join in their singing, having nothing else to do, but enjoying himself; as if by playing in this way he had found a purpose he did not have, or remember having, before.

And then, because so much time had passed, measured perhaps in years, perhaps in decades, he realized that his life, contained in this empty place, would end in the same way that he had arrived, without forethought, as if by chance, his only company the birds that thrived here.

This place was his place now as much as it was their place. And while he couldn't fly or sing as they did, and while they couldn't build fires or cook as he did, they shared this place that gave them life.

Then one day he fell asleep on a soft, comforting grassy knoll and didn't wake up. The birds were curious and landed near him, staring at his body so still in the grass, wondering when he would move. And more birds landed, waiting for the man to move. When he didn't, when they

14

were sure he was dead, for inertness to them meant death, the largest birds, the hunters and scavengers, climbed on top of him and began pecking, tearing off strips of skin and muscle that they swallowed, first gingerly then in haste; for the taste incensed them. Here was a body worth eating, a feast worth gorging on. Soon there were so many birds clamoring over the body, pecking and tearing and ripping, that it didn't take too much time for the outer body, become feed, to vanish, along with the organs.

If anyone else happens upon this place, having forgotten from whence they came, on a journey they had to make—this empty place full of birds that stretches to each horizon and never seems to end—sooner or later they will come to this grassy knoll with its cleansed, white skeleton, the majority of bones in tact; the skeleton still in its final shape. No doubt they will wonder who this man was and if, in time, they will join him. And they will unless they can find their way out, which is something he couldn't.

And whether they do or don't the birds will enrich or engorge them, composing this empty place by the pitch and flapping of wings and their incessant clamorous song.

Next Text

When it came, it came hard and fast; this slow burning that spread through my lower stomach. But when it peaked, sharp and cutting, I doubled over, gasping for breath. Last night, I was reading in my easy chair when the damn thing came on. I dropped the book, laid my forehead on my knees, shivering, and now and then raking my fingernails over the floor. I might be able to endure the spasm. Not possible. The pain came in waves, and when it subsided and I could breathe more freely it returned, smashing in.

The relentless rhythm undid me. Tears fell. I grabbed hold of my ankles for support and moaned. If anyone heard me, I didn't know it. If anyone felt as I did and we could share our pain, I didn't know that either. I was caught with the walls closing in.

When it passed and I sat up, I was spent, anxious that the next onslaught would be worse. Oh it would come; it would come again. So I took my right hand and put it on my stomach. I made a fist and began twisting it in. Either my flesh had turned into another substance— gelatinous, viscid—or I had lost my mind.

I didn't know. I still don't.

First the fist then the wrist sunk into my stomach. I felt around until I touched something small, hard, round. This was the object that caused my pain. I grabbed it, and pulled my hand out. Then I threw the thing into the air where it floated above me, shuddering, spinning to the right, the left, up and down. Finally it stilled.

I reached up and took it between my thumb and index finger; this hard, round thing, this dot in space. And with it I began to trace on the air different shapes.

As if coiling up from a fire in widening arcs, the area above my head became a cone, with all the weight of the air in the cone, swaying unbalanced on its nadir. Then it shattered, black rays skittering up, shards raining down. From its ruined base a parallelogram shimmered, morphing into other shapes: a triangle, hexagram, octagon, dodecahedron; multitudes of shapes become other shapes, some more slowly, some more quickly, some with a blinding flash, others with an effervescent after burn in disruptive parallel spaces whose brief oscillations forged mottled embryo feathers.

Hyperbolic, heterogeneous, the feathers began to define a body beneath them, the body that carried them. And numinous avian bodies evolved from their foraging plumes.

Palpable, impalpable, this whirling ocular fable foliates. Whippoorwills, falcons, hawks, jays, eagles, ravens, ospreys, albatross distend into each other, chaotic palpation from cresting overflow, munificent tetra log in the high auriferous cloud trails where shadows teem and scintillate and pain, the pain that comes when I least expect it, from the earth in the cave of my stomach, from the loam that infiltrates this earth, uncouples its lances and hardens into clashing mineral side show mnemonics.

When it came, I became...

Sparrow-hawk

The sparrow-hawk is a small predatory bird that feeds on smaller birds and rodents too slow to escape from its sharp talons and beak. But what the sparrow-hawk doesn't know or sense is what I do…

Inside the sparrow-hawk is a house. And inside this house is a room where the moon lives, white gray, with five darker circles that are eyes, five dark eyes with gray pinprick irises that gaze out from that room in that house in the center of the sparrow-hawk's body. Now this moon is not the moon in orbit about Earth but a miniature moon that has found its place, the only place it can be for the time I give it, the time it takes, the time we share: me gazing in, it gazing out. And this gazing—which turns inside out and outside in—bears a sea as small as a pebble cast up on a beach by a wave, and as deep as any other sea beyond the room in this house in the center of this sparrow-hawk. And in this sea (low lights, pause) is a forest of kelp, richly green, thickly swaying with the tides and the watery thrum of amphibious birds who resemble the sparrow-hawk, but with gills and oily feathers that prevent them from sinking.

Now all too quickly the scene frays, and the forest of kelp in the sea born from the gaze that we share dissolves. And I am left where I began—with a sparrow-hawk perched on a branch of a large tree fifty years ago when the miniature moon was an enigma fit for someone so young and impressionable. For my eyes then resembled the eyes of the sparrow-hawk just outside on that branch beyond my room in that house in the center of the body of that bird.

There is an infinite progression of complexity here, of course, spatially and temporally. But I leave that to you. Use it as you wish. Just note this: When you see a sparrow-hawk perching on a branch or a fence post or at the top of a chimney searching for prey, in the center of its body is another pulse, not from its heart but from a house with a room where the moon lives, this white gray miniature moon, with five darker circles for eyes and gray pinprick irises whose gaze, if you let it, becomes your own; just as it did for me—in this room with five dark eyes on the surface of that moon in a house in the center of the sparrow-hawk.

Glissando

An anxious, tremulous bowing... The eyes dart right and left, up and down, turning in their sockets to gain from each angle sufficient circular compass. Little can approach unseen... And the tone, if just at the limit of definition, strips from its rhythms a parallel motif that shatters abruptly in truncated stresses and fibrillations; those quick tiny devolving nebulas that stutter in falsetto; minute appeals we sometimes cling to, knowing that the little they do is enough to forestall a greater, suffocating avalanche.

Glissando, which offers chameleon escape...

Bird of Paradise

This bird, so certain myths tell us, was born from the great tropical flower that bears its name, which is native to New Guinea and other nearby islands. Although the myths differ in scope and detail—which we have translated only in part, their song lines much forgotten and their singers rare—they all note that the flower came first, the bird second, and without the flower the bird could never have become what we prize it for: exceptional coloration, intricate mating rituals, and various sizes: diminutive to taller.

So, too, the flower, which ranges from 6 inches to 15 feet in height, with a long stem and leaves similar to, if smaller than, those of the banana tree. Its imposing culmination, the bird-like flower, derives from two elements: an elongated horizontal "beak" of blue feathers at the bottom and a stunning crown or headdress of orange, yellow or white sepias that rise above the beak as if lifting in flight.

One recently found myth that details the origin of the bird also speaks to its antiquity, implicating a landmass prior to the full separation of the island from the Australian continent; its progenitor. That the myth roots in a cultural memory is not an issue. But when that memory arose is.

Because of volcanic activity, earthquakes, lightning storms and flooding rains, the regularity and intensity of which surpass related episodes in the historical record, the flower developed sentience; its way of responding to a world in tumult. Fearing for its inheritance, its life and its future, it sought allies in the night sky; those fiery beings we know as stars. Despite their distance, their radiance and recurrence night after night, year after year would provide for the flower. In order to attract a star, however, the flower had to communicate with it. And so, rooted to the earth, it began to sway with the wind, dipping and bowing in ever-larger circles, petal beak open. The beauty of the flower magnified by its movements pierced the forest cover and spread into the heavens. The star took notice and let drip, in appreciation, a silvery gob of pus, which the flower drank down. The pus engendered an egg in the bloating stem of the flower. From an embryo of sap internal organs grew, wings developed, as did lambent eyes and a feathery skin with brilliant bald patches. When the bird burst from its shell, it killed its mother. Then it flew off.

There is little to distinguish this creation myth from others save one thing. The flower precedes the bird in the same way that one word precedes another.

Size, shape, and coloration:

The Bird of Paradise ranges from near starling to crow-like size and shape. Color intensity and hue (from feather pigment and skin layers that scatter light), along with character of song, enable us to identify one species over another.

Exorbitant tail feather displays (on some species longer than the body), exquisitely delicate antenna-like head plumes, gleaming breastplate iridescence, and decorative web-like wing fans of no practical use other than for visual seduction confirm the bird's uniqueness.

26

When the bird suddenly appears within the thick, humid, forest green in a circle of light formed by a high clearing, we know we have entered a realm where living needs, mask, and costume cohere.

Let us not forget that coloration, and the arch changes a male can provoke by movement in light, compel sexual selection, ensuring a new generation. A bird pair propagates; the species survive. Let us also not forget that the failure rate is high and the effort complex; the lovely but less striking female refusing to acquiesce to a male in full display. That is why males must not only intensify their use of blacks, blues, oranges, reds and aqua, framing transitions when possible—black into blue, orange into red, etc.—they must combine their palette with flamboyant choreographies and transformations of locale. Nothing is too much to snare a mate from the competition, just out of sight.

Mating

Mating rituals root in genetic structure refined by early role-playing and practice. The male locates and secures an available space: an empty low-lying branch or small open area on the forest floor. Its sense of entrance, of how best to attract a female, is perfectly theatrical; the male draws focus entirely to himself.

Some males prepare the space, cleansing it of visual distraction. For those that settle in a small clearing, this can mean two things: using what's available or elaborating a circular or semi-circular performing area rimmed with pebbles. Song introduces the ritual, with brief cries, quick ululations, squawks or sharp whistles. The visual display follows, a rhythmic performance or dance that can include trembling or shimmying as the male steps left to right and right to left on a median across the playing area, puffing out the iridescent breastplate—at times nearly to occlude the head—and extending the wings, or wing fans, with their changing coloration to forefront the male's qualities: strength, endurance or attractiveness. If on a branch the mating dance can mean turning, revolving or bobbing, bending suddenly forward so that feathers pour over the head, slowly flapping one wing, or wing fan, then another, and similar gestures. There is little doubt that the male seeks to induce in the female a kind of hypnosis that impels seduction.

If the male is successful and the female chooses him, she makes that known through touch. Beyond the hypnotic effect of the dance is the recognition that this male alone is for her. What finally clinches the choice is not something we have determined. Nonetheless, with attractiveness a premiere quality throughout the ritual, it is easy to equate it with beauty; a sense of beauty similar to our own that the female possesses and the male emblazons. In this way, the female chooses a mate by the esthetic tenor and largess of his appeal, which gathers within it other qualities based on aggressiveness.

Habitat:

Low mountainous and swampy areas, seemingly incommensurate, comprise the usual habitat for this bird. What we might forget when documenting each habitat individually is how the contrast between them plays out for us and, more precisely, how we embellish it: in effect, the bird can thrive in realms that suggestion creates.

As an old tale has it, the bird has no feet, evolution having dispensed with them, and lives in flight, buoyed by air currents formed by surface heating. It only lands when death is near. Although we know this for what it is, a misperception sparked by wonder, it speaks to the genius and subtlety of this bird, which behavioral data cannot encompass.

As if come from another extravagant world, the Bird of Paradise trains our fascination and transforms it. And from that point on we are its prey, seeking ourselves through it...

Predation:

The bird is an omnivore, feeding on insects and fruit with sips of sweet flowery nectar for refreshment. It does not prey on other birds, small mammals or fish.

Nesting:

The bird uses branch forks in trees to build its nest in, woven from soft leaves, tendrils, and other kinds of humus. The number of eggs, from one to three, varies with species size. What does not vary is the gentle, nebulous luminosity emanating from the egg, which expresses, both in shadow and sunlight, the coming coloration of the mature bird.

Migration:

The bird lives in the habitats it is born into, having no need to migrate; except of course to realms that we envision in tribute to its beauty, its self-possession of such, and our desire to express the same, whenever and however we can.

Kassandra Bird

The Kassandra Bird is named after the young princess and prophetess that King Agamemnon, victorious at Troy, returns home with; now his slave and concubine.

It is Apollo who has exalted Kassandra with the gift of prophecy. But the gift is double edged, and cuts both ways: vision, disbelief then murder. What she can see, smell and hear that others cannot; this disembodied, demonic arc of their future...

Not only is there nothing she can do to make her captors accept her prophecy and prevent the acts she relates, those fateful deeds to come, they fear her. How can they endure this woman for whom time is transparent; who thrashes, shrieks and foams to cull from the air the words she utters?

They cannot. They turn against her.

They thrust their blades into her chest.

*

The bird enfolds the tale, repeating it and again. It is not so much a song as a shriek from bass to soprano, ripping apart the resonance that grounds it with a last bloody strand lifting up and dying off.

The shriek not the bird remains, the shriek that gives the bird its name: eyes stark, a thin lattice of spit drying on its beak, the leaves around it spattered, mute witness to an exploded wreck.

*

The Kassandra Bird preys on insects, smaller birds and mammals, snakes, lizards, whatever it can kill, whatever is available, including mineral-rich plants from the Amaranth family.

When larger birds hunt it down and escape is impossible, it resorts to a kind of mimicry. The body stiffens; a rank odor of putrefaction diffuses through the feathers; the irises turn gray.

The skill and speed of the change confuses the predator. Hungry for warm meat but repulsed by the smell, it pecks at the hard, tasteless body. Unless its kill is fresh, it doesn't eat. It soon gives up and flies off. A minute or two later the Kassandra Bird softens and warms.

*

The Kassandra Bird flies into the high reaches of the avian sky, which most birds must avoid or asphyxiate. It does this by catalyzing in its lungs an added value to the oxygen it has breathed in. Friction from microscopic cilia produces the spark, which also keeps body temperature stable. Reports place its ceiling at around 35,000 feet.

At that height, the Kassandra Bird normally flies alone, above yet tied to the fray below it. We have yet to establish the reason why the bird flies so high other than that it does. Perhaps the simple freedom of knowing there are few competitors is a deciding factor. Perhaps it is the pleasure derived from this freedom. When it returns to Earth, it replenishes, first drinking then eating.

*

Mating is at night, with preference given to the darker periods of the new moon when shadows are faint. Oddly, initiation of the mating ritual and choice are the reverse of other birds. The female begins the ritual by subtle modulations in her screech that opens a deeper rhythmic tone that males can hear but which humans can barely discern. Young males, usually no more than several, follow the tone to the branch where the female perches.

Smell and wingspan are key. As the female smells her suitors, from beak to tail feathers, lingering over the pungent breast, they spread their wings. The more seductive the male smell is, the broader the wingspan. Having made her choice, the female then pushes the other males off the branch. If a male challenges her, she pecks at him until he exits. The chosen male and the female screech in counterpoint; their interior modulations variably synced. They mate and begin to build their nest.

The reverse of roles in sexual selection refers the bird to the ancient tragedy. For while the prophetess reveals the murders to come, including her murder, without that revelation the acts turn sordid and petty. Hatred of husband and revenge for a daughter's sacrifice that launched a war does not become tragedy on its own.

*

The Kassandra Bird has well adapted to two geographies across Africa and Central and South America: open savannahs and tropical forests. Although its place of origin and evidence of migration are insufficiently known, researchers agree that the bird thrives where it lives. And while its total population is low compared to other birds, its sinister defense against predators and singular biology when flying at height secures its continuity.

Humans are the only predators that can kill the bird at will. And for this bird, humans are as gods: Apollo, Zeus and Hades combined.

This is one reason why the bird fears humans and keeps its distance. It may also be the reason why the bird appears in several ancient myths that confer on it prophetic abilities.

Kassandra—bird and Trojan prophetess, whose prescience resides in her voice...

Allan Graubard's poems, fiction, theater works, and literary and theater criticism are published or performed in the U.S., Canada, Brazil, Chile, U.K., and the E.U., with translation into numerous languages. He has appeared as reader, guest artist, and lecturer at venues, large and small, from MoMA PS1, the Strasberg Theater & Film Institute, Cornelia Street Cafe (New York) to Garden Street Bookshop (New Orleans) and Cite des Arts (Lafayette, Louisiana), Beyond Baroque (Los Angeles), Wesleyan University (Connecticut), McGill University (Montreal), October Gallery (London), University of Oxford, in Dubrovnik (Croatia), Sarajevo (Bosnia Herzegovina), and elsewhere.

His books include: *Western Terrace*, *A Crescent by Any Other Name*, *Targets*, *And Tell Tulip the Summer*, *Roma Amor*, *Fragments from Nomad Days*, *Ascent of Sublime Love*, and more. He is editor of and contributing author to *Into the Mylar Chamber: Ira Cohen, Invisible Heads: Surrealists in North America – An Untold Story* (with Thom Burns), and co-editor and contributing author to *The Art of Conduction: Conduction Workbook,* by Lawrence D. "Butch" Morris.

His theater works include, among others: *For Alejandra, Woman Bomb/Sade*, and with Lawrence D. "Butch" Morris, *Modette and Erotic Eulogy.*

He lives in New York with his wife, Carolyn McGee.

Rik Lina has lived and worked on different continents preferably in wild nature, as a way of life, led by Odilon Redon's advice: "Immerse yourself in nature!" He dedicated his life and art to study the deserts, mountains, tropical rainforests, and coral reef jungles. In 1975, he began scuba diving in earnest off the Caribbean Island of Bonaire, and from the shores of several other countries, logging over 1000 hours underwater. A majority of his drawing, painting and graphic art represents the poetry and life of the pelagic realms, along with his explorations of jungles, of cloud forests, always in connection with inner space.

After studies at the Rietveld Academy of Amsterdam, Rik Lina made countless individual and collective international exhibitions. In 1968, his collaborations with surrealist poets begin in different periodicals: *Brumes Blondes,* edited by Laurens Vancrevel, and the periodicals associated with *Movement Phases,* led by Edouard Jaguer. Rik Lina founded the anarchist/surrealist periodical, *Droomschaar* (1990-1994), where he met Allan Graubard. He is also co-founder of several international collective painting initiatives: *CAPA—Collective Automatic Painting Amsterdam* (since 1991), the *Cabo Mondego Section of Portuguese Surrealism* (since 2008), and *Cornucopia* (since 2010).

Since 2007, Rik Lina divides his time between his studios in Figueira da Foz, Portugal, and Amsterdam, The Netherlands.

Acknowledgments

I wish to thank Thom Burns for his design expertise, my wife and companion in bird land, Carolyn McGee, and all those for whom birds are an inducement for dreaming with eyes open.

www.ingramcontent.com/pod-product-compliance
Lightning Source LLC
Chambersburg PA
CBHW060810270326

41928CB00002B/41